Beyond the Wall

Study Guide

A Reader's Companion to
Don't Be Just Another Brick in the Wall

Dirrick L. Williams, Sr.

This guide is intended for educational and personal development use. It is not a substitute for clinical mental health care, counseling, therapy, or other professional services.

Individuals may choose to use this material for personal reflection and independent study. It is recommended that this study guide/companion be used in a group setting, ideally supported and guided by a licensed, certified, or registered **Beyond The Wall Facilitator.**

No person may facilitate, lead, teach, or provide services of, or related to, *"Don't Be Just Another Brick In The Wall," "Beyond The Wall Study Guide,"* or *"Beyond The Wall Facilitator's Guide,"* or any associated teachings or modalities, without an official license, certification, or express written permission mutually agreed upon by the publisher, author, or their corporately designated and authorized representatives.

For information regarding becoming a **Beyond The Wall Facilitator** or an official **Beyond The Wall Partner,** contact us at:

www.dirrickwilliams.com

Dedication

To every person who has ever felt
unseen, unheard, or misunderstood—
May these pages help you discover the truth of who you are.

Epigraph

"The moment you stop accepting the story others write and tell of you,

is the moment you begin to write your own story."

For

Janelle Grace Garza
Wesley Kennath Richardson

TABLE OF CONTENTS

PREFACE

There are moments in life when we feel as though we are placed, shaped, or limited by forces we did not choose. We follow patterns we never questioned, repeat beliefs we never examined, and live behind emotional walls that were built long before we understood our own identity.

This guide is your invitation to step out from behind those walls.

Don't Be Just Another Brick in the Wall began as a journey of self-discovery, but it has become something more—an opportunity for every reader to pause, reflect, and reclaim the truth of who they are.

This companion guide is your personal space to explore:

- The messages you received growing up
- The beliefs you formed along the way
- The emotional defenses you built
- The identity you've carried, worn, or hidden
- The parts of you still waiting to be expressed

No matter where you are reading this—from a quiet home, a meeting room, or a correctional facility—this guide belongs to you. It is a space where honesty, courage, and transformation are welcome.

You are not required to share these pages with anyone.

You do not need to perform or impress.

This is your journey. Your truth. Your next chapter.

A Note From the Author

Before you begin, I want to acknowledge something important:

You have already demonstrated courage simply by opening this guide.

Self-reflection is not easy. It asks you to be honest with yourself in ways that the world does not always make room for. Honesty with yourself is the beginning of freedom. It is the first Step toward discovering the life you were meant to live rather than the life others shaped for you.

As you work through each session:

- Take your time
- Breathe deeply
- Honor your past
- Respect your story
- And remember that change begins the moment you decide to see yourself clearly.

My hope is that this guide becomes a companion on your journey, not a teacher telling you who to be, but a mirror showing you the greatness of who you truly are.

—Dirrick L. Williams

How To Use This Guide

This guide is structured to help you uncover your own truth at your own pace.

Each session includes:

- A brief introduction
- A key teaching from the chapter
- Reflection questions for personal insight
- A private exercise designed for your own transformation
- A one-sentence breakthrough statement

You Do NOT Need:

- A group
- A facilitator
- To write perfectly
- To share your answers with anyone

You only need:

- Honesty
- Willingness
- Time with yourself

Important: There is no right or wrong answer. There is only your answer. Your truth. Your moment of seeing yourself more clearly.

Keep in mind that truth is experienced in a relationship. Therefore, we recommend this experience be shared with groups and certified facilitators, though this is not required.

Your Commitment to Yourself

Before you begin, take a moment to make a personal commitment. Read the following aloud, or silently, with intention:

"I will be honest with myself in these pages.
I will show up for myself.
I will explore my story with courage and compassion."

Sign or initial if you choose:

Signature: _________________________

Date: _____________________________

THE CLICHÉ

Stepping Out of Automatic Living

INTRODUCTION

There are moments in life when a single sentence, even one spoken casually, carries a truth that follows us for years. In this session, you will explore how expectations, roles, and unspoken rules shaped your early life, and how those influences may still affect you today.

"The Cliché" is not just a phrase. It is an invitation.

It asks you to consider whether the life you are living is truly your own, or whether it was built for you long before you knew you had a choice.

This is where your journey begins.

*Living from the past, or
living for the future?*

In the book, a frustrated teenager leaves home, and her father calls out:

"Don't be just another brick in the wall!"

That line awakens something in the narrator.
It sparks reflection.
It stirs a question he can no longer ignore.

He begins to recognize that much of life is shaped by:

- Expectations placed on us
- The habits we inherited
- The fears we absorbed
- The roles we learned to play

And he realizes something important:

> *Before we live the life we shape for ourselves,*
> *We live a life shaped by others.*

This session invites you to uncover where that may be true in your own life.

Reflection Questions

Take your time. Answer honestly. Write as much or as little as you choose.

1. Growing up, what was one expectation placed on you that shaped how you saw yourself?

____

____

2. Were you ever pushed into a role, spoken or unspoken, that you did not choose? What was that role?

____

____

3. When you think about your childhood or teenage years, whose voice felt like they were pulling the strings?

____

____

4. What did those voices teach you about who you *"should"* be?

____

____

5. Do you feel you have lived more by choice or by habit? Explain.

____

____

6. What part of your life feels automatic, as if it came from someone else's blueprint?

____

____

Personal Exercise
"Name Your Wall"

This exercise is meant for you alone. Find a quiet moment to reflect.

Step 1: Complete this sentence:

"The wall I have lived behind is…"

Examples:

- "Trying to be strong all the time."
- "Acting like I don't care."
- "Doing what other people expected."
- "Hiding my real feelings."
- "Pretending nothing bothers me."

Step 2: Answer this question honestly:

"I built this wall because…"

Finish the sentence, even if the answer surprises you.

____

____

____

____

____

____

STEP 3: REFLECTION:

Write a few lines about how this wall protected you, and how it limited you.

You do not need to show this to anyone unless you choose to.

This is your truth, for your eyes only.

____

____

____

____

____

____

____

____

____

____

____

____

____

____

____

____

____

____

Your Breakthrough Statement

At the end of each session, you will choose one sentence that captures your personal insight.

For Session 1, use this prompt:

"One part of my life I no longer want shaped by others is…"

Write your statement here:

____

____

____

____

____

____

____

____

____

____

____

____

____

____

This sentence becomes your anchor for the week.

THE QUEST

Beginning the Search for Meaning

INTRODUCTION

Every journey toward change begins with a moment of curiosity, a feeling inside you that says, ***"There has to be more than this."***

In this session, you will explore the early sparks of your own quest: the questions, experiences, and inner shifts that led you to seek something deeper in your life.

In the book, the narrator searches for a brick wall.
Not because a wall has answers, but because ***he is finally ready to ask questions.***

Your quest may look different, but the feeling is the same:
A desire to understand who you are... and who you are becoming.

This session invites you to honor that desire.

> *The gift of a good answer is*
> *the ability to ask better questions.*
>
> *When did you stop asking questions?*

When the narrator first approaches the wall, he feels awkward and uncertain about what he is doing. But something inside drives him to keep going.

He asks the wall a simple question:

"What does it mean not to be just another brick in the wall?"

At first, nothing happens.
But then he realizes something important. The wall does not speak first. The seeker does.

The moment you begin searching, answers begin to appear.

Sometimes quietly.
Sometimes unexpectedly.
But always in response to your willingness to look inward.

This chapter teaches:

> *Your quest does not begin with finding answers.*
> *It begins with **wanting the truth**.*

Reflection Questions

Reflect honestly. Let your answers reveal what they need to.

1. What moment or experience in your life made you start seeking deeper meaning?

____

____

2. Have you ever felt pulled toward something without fully understanding why? Describe it.

____

____

3. What questions about your life have followed you for years?

____

____

4. What have you been afraid to ask yourself until now?

____

____

5. What kind of change do you secretly hope is possible for you?

____

____

6. What part of your inner world feels ready to be explored?

____

____

Personal Exercise
"The Question Within"

This exercise helps you uncover the deeper question beneath your search for change.

Step 1: Write down the first question you remember asking about your life.

(From childhood, teenage years, or adulthood.)

Examples:
- "Why am I like this?"
- "Why does this keep happening?"
- "What am I supposed to be doing with my life?"
- "Why do I feel this way?"

Step 2: Now go deeper.

Ask yourself:

"What question am I really asking beneath that first question?"

Take your time.
Often, the real question is more emotional, more personal, and more meaningful.

____

____

____

____

STEP 3: FINISH THIS STATEMENT:

"The real question I am searching for in my life right now is..."

Write your answer slowly, allowing honesty to guide your words.

____

____

____

____

____

____

____

____

____

____

____

____

YOUR BREAKTHROUGH STATEMENT

Choose a sentence that reflects what you discovered in this session.

Use this prompt:

"Today, I honor my desire to search for truth by asking..."

Write your sentence here:

____

____

____

____

____

____

____

____

____

____

____

____

____

____

____

____

____

This becomes your guiding question until the next session.

THE FOUNDATION

Understanding the Ground You Stand On

INTRODUCTION

Every life is built on a foundation of beliefs, experiences, memories, relationships, and messages that sink into us long before we understand how deeply they shape who we become.

- Some foundations are strong.
- Some are cracked.
- Some were built by people who loved us.
- Others were built by people who hurt us.
- All of them influence how we see ourselves and how we move through life.

This session invites you to explore your foundation with honesty and compassion.

> *Before you can build anything new in your life, you must understand the ground you're building upon.*

In the book, the wall teaches that:

"Purity and transparency do not exist alone.
They are revealed through your interactions with others."

The narrator learns that:

- We are influenced every moment by the world around us.
- Our reactions are shaped by history, environment, habits, and desires.
- Our expression of self is affected by what we carry, seen and unseen.

The most important lesson of this chapter is:

Your foundation is not just what happened to you. It's how you have learned to relate to yourself and others because of it.

> *"What matters most as you share who you are is not what you share, but the awareness of self as you share."*

Reflection Questions

Let these questions guide you deeper into your personal history.

1. When you think about your early life, what beliefs were you taught about yourself?

____

____

2. What emotions or reactions have followed you from childhood into adulthood?

____

____

3. Who were the people whose words or behaviors shaped your sense of worth?

____

____

4. What circumstances from your past still influence how you respond to others today?

____

____

5. What part of your foundation feels steady? What part feels unstable?

____

____

6. If your foundation had a *"message"* written on it, what would that message be?

____

____

Personal Exercise
"Mapping Your Foundation"

This exercise helps you identify the emotional and psychological ground you've been standing on your whole life.

Step 1: Draw a simple outline of a foundation or base (even just a rectangle).

Inside it, write three words that describe what your early foundation felt like.

Examples:

- "Uncertain"
- "Controlled"
- "Loved"
- "Chaotic"
- "Strict"
- "Unstable"
- "Hopeful"

Choose whatever feels true.

STEP 2: BELOW THE FOUNDATION, WRITE THIS SENTENCE:

"How my foundation still affects me today..."

Write freely for a few minutes. Notice what comes up.

____

____

____

____

____

____

____

STEP 3: ABOVE YOUR FOUNDATION, WRITE THIS QUESTION:

"What kind of foundation do I want to build now?"

You do not need all the answers yet.

You only need the willingness to see clearly.

____

____

____

____

____

____

____

____

____

____

____

Your Breakthrough Statement

Choose one sentence that honors your growing self-awareness.

Use this prompt:

"Today, I acknowledge the foundation I came from, and I am ready to build…"

Write your statement here:

____

____

____

____

____

____

____

____

____

____

____

____

____

____

This becomes your guiding awareness for the week.

Session 4

The Meaning

The Difference Between Expression and Protection

Introduction

Much of what we believe is ***"self-expression"*** is actually ***self-protection***. A mask, a defense, or a role we learned to play so we wouldn't be hurt, rejected, or exposed.

This session helps you explore the difference between:

- The you the world sees
- The you that exists beneath the layers of fear, pride, pain, and survival

You will explore the masks you've worn, the reasons you wore them, and the parts of you that were buried or silenced in the process.

- This is a session of honesty.
- This is a session of courage.
- It is a session of reclaiming your true voice.

> *To lose your voice is to wander through life, aimlessly.*

Insights

In the book, the narrator hesitates to speak to the wall, not because he doesn't know what to say, but because the truth he wants to express feels uncomfortable.

The wall teaches him that:

"You are seldom the first to hear your deepest expression.
You are the last, because you've been hiding it beneath layers."

This chapter reveals that:

- Our "identity" is often a shield.
- Fear and shame shape our voices.
- We learn to express only what feels safe.
- True expression requires vulnerability, awareness, and acceptance.

The meaning behind the wall's lesson is simple but powerful:

To express yourself fully, you must first recognize what you have been protecting.

Answer with honesty. Take your time.

1. What is one *"mask"* you learned to wear growing up?

____

____

2. What did that mask protect you from? (Examples: judgment, pain, embarrassment, weakness.)

____

____

3. What part of your real self has been hidden behind that mask?

____

____

4. How has self-protection shaped your relationships?

____

____

5. What is one truth you rarely speak out loud?

____

____

6. What would expressing your true self allow you to feel?

____

____

PERSONAL EXERCISE
"THE MASK I WEAR, THE VOICE I HIDE"

This exercise helps you name the difference between who you've shown the world and who you really are inside.

STEP 1: COMPLETE THIS SENTENCE:

"The mask I wear is…"

Examples:

- "the tough guy"
- "the quiet one"
- "the one who doesn't care"
- "the strong one"
- "the entertainer"
- "the unbreakable one"

Write what feels true.

____

____

____

____

____

____

____

____

____

STEP 2: NOW COMPLETE THIS SENTENCE:

"The voice I hide is..."

Examples:

- ➤ "I'm hurting."

- ➤ "I feel alone."

- ➤ "I'm afraid."

- ➤ "I want something better."

- ➤ "I miss being myself."

- ➤ "I don't know who I am anymore."

Let the answer come naturally.

____

____

____

____

____

____

____

____

____

____

STEP 3: REFLECTION

Write 6–10 lines answering:

"What did my mask protect me from, and what did it cost me?"

Be gentle with yourself. This realization is powerful.

YOUR BREAKTHROUGH STATEMENT

Use this prompt:

"I acknowledge the mask I've worn, and I am ready to reclaim..."

Write your statement here:

____

____

____

____

____

____

____

____

____

____

____

____

____

____

____

____

This becomes your grounding truth for the week.

THE RATIONALE

Understanding Why You Became Who You Became

INTRODUCTION

Every behavior has a reason.
Every reaction has a history.

Every mask, wall, and emotional pattern was created to meet a need, whether that need was safety, acceptance, control, survival, or belonging.

This session helps you explore the **"why"** behind your choices, roles, defenses, and identity.

Clarity creates compassion.
Compassion creates change.

> *You are not examining your past to judge yourself.*
> *You are examining it to understand yourself.*

In the chapter, the narrator attempts to justify his behavior to the wall.

He offers explanations, excuses, and familiar stories. But the wall responds in a way that challenges him. It refuses to accept the story at face value.:

This chapter teaches that:

- Not everything we call a *"reason"* is the real reason.
- We often build our identity around survival responses.
- We explain our behavior based on what we feared, not what we truly wanted.
- Understanding the real motive behind our actions unlocks possibilities and change.

The wall pushes the narrator to examine the deeper rationale beneath his patterns.

Now it's your turn.

> *"What you call a reason may only be a reaction*
> *you repeated until it felt like truth."*

Answer at your own pace. Be honest with yourself.

1. Think of one behavior you've repeated for years. What did you believe was the *"reason"* for it?

____

____

2. What deeper need, or fear, may have actually driven that behavior?

____

____

3. Who or what taught you to react that way?

____

____

4. How has this pattern impacted your relationships or opportunities?

____

____

5. Has this *"reason"* protected you, limited you, or both? Explain.

____

____

6. What new understanding about yourself is beginning to emerge?

____

____

Personal Exercise
"The Real Reason"

This exercise helps you look beneath your explanations and discover the deeper truth.

Step 1: Choose one pattern in your life.

Examples:

- Acting tough
- Avoiding emotions
- Anger
- Isolation
- People-pleasing
- Distrust
- Self-sabotage

Write it at the top of your page.

Step 2: Answer this question:

"What did I tell myself about why I did this?"

Write the surface explanation.

____

____

____

____

____

STEP 3: NOW DIG DEEPER. ASK YOURSELF:

"What was the real reason beneath the reason?"

Examples:

- "I didn't want to look weak."
- "I was afraid of being abandoned."
- "I didn't trust myself."
- "I wanted to feel in control."
- "I didn't believe I deserved good things."
- "I was trying to protect my heart."

Let the truth show itself gently.

STEP 4: REFLECTION

Write a few sentences on how this new understanding changes the way you see yourself.

____

____

____

____

____

____

____

____

____

____

____

____

____

____

____

____

____

____

____

Your Breakthrough Statement

Use this prompt:

"I now understand that beneath my behavior was a need for…"

Write your insight here:

____

____

____

____

____

____

____

____

____

____

____

____

____

____

This becomes your guiding clarity for the week.

THE AWAKENING

Seeing Yourself with New Eyes

INTRODUCTION

Every meaningful journey has a moment when something inside you shifts.
A moment when you begin to see your life, your patterns, and your identity more clearly.

This moment is called ***awakening***.

Awakening doesn't mean everything suddenly makes sense.
It means you are finally aware enough to start asking different questions:

1. "Is this who I want to be?"

2. "Does this belief still serve me?"

3. "What else is possible for my life?"

This session leads you into a deeper awareness of who you truly are beneath the fears, habits, and defenses you've carried for years.

> *Awakening is the doorway to transformation.*

In this chapter, the narrator begins to sense that something is changing, not outside of him, but within him. The wall challenges him to see that the world hasn't suddenly shifted…

He has.

Awakening begins internally before it appears externally.

This chapter shows that awakening is:

- A new awareness of the self
- A deeper honesty about your past
- A desire to look inward rather than outward
- A recognition of your power and responsibility

Awakening is not dramatic.
It is quiet, steady, and deeply personal.

Awakening is the process and the moment when you stop running from yourself.

"When you awaken, you stop living from the surface and start listening from within."

Go slowly. Let self-awareness guide you.

1. Have you ever felt a moment in your life where something inside shifted? Describe it.

____

____

2. What truths about yourself are becoming clearer to you now?

____

____

3. What beliefs or assumptions are you beginning to question?

____

____

4. What part of your identity feels like it is waking up or coming alive?

____

____

5. How does it feel to see yourself more honestly?

____

____

6. What do you believe awakening is asking of you right now?

____

____

Personal Exercise
"The Moment I Woke Up"

This exercise helps you explore your personal awakening moment, or the moment that may be happening right now.

Step 1: Complete this sentence:

"A moment in my life when I began to wake up was…"

It may be:

A loss
A mistake
A relationship
A conversation
A time when you felt broken
A time when you felt inspired
Or a moment of complete honesty

Whatever it is, trust it.

Step 2: Finish this sentence:

"That moment taught me that I needed to…"

Write freely and without judgment.

____

____

____

Answer this in 5–7 sentences:

"What is awakening in me right now, and what does it mean for my future?"

Let the truth rise gently.

Awakening is not about perfection. It is about awareness.

Your Breakthrough Statement

Use this prompt:

"Today I honor my awakening by choosing to…"

Write your statement here:

____

____

____

____

____

____

____

____

____

____

____

____

____

____

This becomes your guiding intention for the week.

THE CHANGE

Accepting the Need to Become Someone New

INTRODUCTION

Awakening leads you to an important realization:

Something in your life must change. Awareness demands response.

- Not because you are broken.
- Not because you failed.

But because the way you have lived so far no longer aligns with the truth you are discovering about yourself.

In this session, you will explore the changes your inner growth is calling you toward, and the fears and hopes that come with it.

> *Change is not about forcing a new identity. It is about releasing the patterns, beliefs, and emotional habits that once felt necessary but now feel heavy, limiting, or untrue.*

In this chapter, the narrator realizes that when you awaken, you can no longer pretend not to see.

The wall teaches him:

"Once you are aware, you cannot return to being unaware. That is the beginning of change."

The wall challenges him to stop telling the same stories...and start creating new ones.

This chapter reveals:

- Awareness creates accountability.
- Accountability creates possibility.
- Possibility creates transformation.

> *Change is not about fixing the past—it is about shaping the future with clarity and intention.*

Allow your answers to be honest, gentle, and rooted in awareness.

1. What is one thing in your life you know needs to change?

____

____

2. What part of you has been asking for that change the longest?

____

____

3. What fear has held you back from changing sooner?

____

____

4. What might your life look like if you fully embraced this change?

____

____

5. Who would you become if you stopped repeating old patterns?

____

____

6. What inner strength is waking up in you right now?

____

____

Personal Exercise
"The Change I'm Called To"

This exercise helps you identify the specific change your awakening is pointing toward.

Step 1: Complete this sentence:

"The change I need to make in my life is…"

This may be:

- Emotional
- Behavioral
- Relational
- Internal
- Spiritual
- Or something else entirely

There is no wrong answer.

____

____

____

____

____

____

____

____

STEP 2: ANSWER THIS QUESTION HONESTLY:

"What is the fear behind this change?"

Examples:

- Fear of failing
- Fear of looking weak
- Fear of being alone
- Fear of being judged
- Fear of being misunderstood
- Fear of losing control

____

____

____

____

____

____

____

____

____

STEP 3: NOW FINISH THIS SENTENCE:

"If I choose this change, I will gain..."

Focus on what will grow in you: clarity, peace, honesty, strength, purpose.

____

____

____

____

STEP 4: REFLECTION

Write 4–6 lines about why this change matters to your life and identity.

____

____

____

____

____

____

____

____

____

____

____

____

Your Breakthrough Statement

Use this prompt:

"Today I accept that change is necessary because..."

Write your insight here:

____

____

____

____

____

____

____

____

____

____

____

____

____

Let this become your affirmation until the next session.

THE PRIORITY

Choosing What Matters Most Now

INTRODUCTION

Once you recognize that change is necessary, the next question is:

"What should I prioritize first?"

Life becomes clearer when you begin to separate, since clarity requires distinction:

- What truly matters
- From what you only tolerated
- From what was expected of you
- From what no longer belongs

In this session, you will explore what deserves your time, attention, energy, and commitment at this stage of your life.

You are not choosing what mattered in the past.
You are choosing what matters now.

In this chapter, the wall guides the narrator to understand that awakening leads to clarity, and clarity leads to focus.

The wall says:

"Your life becomes what you give your attention to."

The narrator realizes:

1. Some priorities were never really his.

2. Some habits were inherited.

3. Some responsibilities were chosen out of fear, not purpose.

4. Some values were reactions, not decisions.

When you decide what matters most, you begin shaping the life you are meant to live.

> *Your true priorities reveal your true identity.*

Let these questions help you discover what deserves your focus.

1. What have you given most of your energy to in the past?

____

____

2. Which of those things actually mattered to your growth or well-being?

____

____

3. What have you been neglecting that deserves more of your attention now?

____

____

4. What do you want your life to stand for at this stage?

____

____

5. What values feel the most important to you today?

____

____

6. What would your life look like if your priorities were aligned with your truth?

____

____

Personal Exercise
"What Matters Most Now"

This exercise helps you identify the priorities that will guide your next chapter.

Step 1: Make two short lists:

List A: Things I used to prioritize.

(Examples: image, survival, anger, approval, control, avoidance)

____

____

____

____

List B: Things I want to prioritize now.

(Examples: honesty, growth, peace, responsibility, healing, purpose)

____

____

____

____

STEP 2: COMPARE THE LISTS.

Write a few lines answering:

"How are my old priorities different from the ones I want today?"

____

____

____

____

____

STEP 3: CHOOSE ONE PRIORITY THAT FEELS THE MOST IMPORTANT.

____

____

____

____

____

STEP 4: REFLECTION

Answer this question in 3–6 sentences:

"How will my life change if I consistently honor this new priority?"

Let your answer come from the place of awakening inside you.

Your Breakthrough Statement

Use this prompt:

"My new priority is ______________________________
 because I am becoming..."

Write your insight here:

____

____

____

____

____

____

____

____

____

____

____

____

____

____

This becomes your guiding focus for the week.

THE APPRAISAL

Evaluating Your Life with Honesty and Compassion

INTRODUCTION

Once you know what matters, the next step is to evaluate where you truly stand.

This process is called **appraisal**, not judgment, not shame, not regret, but evaluation.

Appraisal is not about looking at your life and saying, *"I failed,"* or *"I should have done better."* Instead, it is about saying:

**"This is where I am. This is how I got here.
And this is what I want to change next."**

This session helps you examine the condition of your emotional, mental, spiritual, and relational life with clarity and compassion. You cannot transform what you refuse to examine.

> *You cannot rebuild a life you refuse to look at.*

In this chapter, the narrator learns that appraisal is not about punishment.

The wall teaches:

"Growth requires awareness of what is true, not what you wish were true."

The narrator begins to understand:

- He must take inventory of his life.
- He must face habits he ignored.
- He must confront beliefs he outgrew.
- He must acknowledge emotions he avoided.

The wall teaches that seeing your ***life clearly is an act of courage, not weakness.***

Appraisal is the moment you stop lying to yourself.

Be gentle with yourself. Honesty is not meant to harm you; it is meant to free you.

1. What part of your life feels healthy and aligned right now?

____

____

2. What part of your life feels neglected or out of balance?

____

____

3. What habits or patterns are holding you back the most?

____

____

4. What relationships or influences have shaped your decisions (for better or worse)?

____

____

5. What emotions have you avoided, and how have they affected your life?

____

____

6. What strengths are you beginning to recognize in yourself?

____

____

Personal Exercise
"My Life Appraisal"

This exercise helps you evaluate your life honestly without shame.

Step 1: Draw four short headings on a page:

- Emotional
- Mental
- Relational
- Direction/Purpose

Under each, write one or two sentences describing how that area of your life feels right now.

Examples:

- "My emotions feel heavy but clearer."
- "Mentally, I'm becoming more aware."
- "My relationships feel distant but hopeful."
- "I'm still searching for direction."

Emotional	Mental	Relational	Direction/Purpose

STEP 2: WRITE THIS QUESTION BENEATH YOUR FOUR AREAS:

"What area needs my attention the most right now?"

Write your answer clearly.

____

____

____

____

____

____

____

____

____

____

____

____

____

____

____

____

____

"If I give attention to this area, how will my life begin to change?"

(Answer this in 4–6 sentences)

Let the truth guide you.

____

____

____

____

Your Breakthrough Statement

Use this prompt:

"I choose to see myself clearly because..."

Write your insight here:

____

____

____

____

____

____

____

____

____

____

____

____

____

____

This becomes your guiding clarity for the week.

The Illusion

Questioning the Stories You Have Believed About Yourself

Introduction

So much of our suffering comes from living inside illusions, stories we accepted as truth because they were repeated, familiar, or spoken by people who had influence over us.

Illusions feel real.
Illusions feel safe.
Illusions feel permanent.

But illusions also

limit you,
hide your true identity, and
prevent you from seeing your power clearly.

This session is an opportunity to examine the illusions that shaped your life and to begin untangling yourself from the false stories you once believed.

Illusion ends where awareness begins.

INSIGHTS

In the story, the narrator is confronted by the wall's challenge:

To recognize not only what he believes, but why he believes it.

Illusion dissolves when you shine awareness on it. What you question loses its control over you.

This chapter reveals that:

> ➤ Some beliefs were inherited.

> ➤ Some fears were taught.

> ➤ Some limitations were handed down.

> ➤ Some identities were survival strategies, not truth.

The narrator realizes that awakening requires the courage to question everything that once felt certain.

> *"What you call truth may only be the loudest illusion you learned to obey."*

Reflection Questions

These questions help uncover the beliefs that shaped your identity.

1. What is one belief you carried for years that you now realize may not be true?

____

____

2. Who (or what) taught you that belief?

____

____

3. How did that belief influence your decisions or self-worth?

____

____

4. What emotion rises when you question this belief?

____

____

5. What might be possible for you if this belief were no longer part of your identity?

____

____

6. What new truth is beginning to reveal itself to you?

____

____

Personal Exercise
"The Illusion I Question"

This exercise helps you challenge the stories that shaped your identity.

Step 1: Write down one illusion you believed about yourself.

Examples:

- "I'm not good enough."
- "I have to be strong all the time."
- "I can't trust anyone."
- "People like me don't succeed."
- "I'm defined by my past."

Write whatever feels most true.

____

____

____

____

____

____

____

____

"Where did this belief come from?"

Write the source honestly, even if it's painful.

____

____

____

____

____

____

____

____

____

____

____

____

____

____

____

____

"How has this belief protected me?"

Illusions often begin as emotional armor.

____

____

____

____

____

____

____

____

____

____

____

____

____

____

STEP 4: FINALLY:

"How has this belief limited me?"

(Write 4–6 lines.)

This step brings truth into the open.

Your Breakthrough Statement

Use this prompt:

I release the illusion that

____

____

____

because I now know...

This becomes your guiding affirmation for the week.

THE LECTURE

Recognizing the Influences That Shaped You

INTRODUCTION

Every person is shaped by influences: parents, culture, environment, trauma, friends, teachers, role models, enemies, circumstances, and the silent expectations of the world around us.

- Some influences guide us.
- Some distort us
- Some protect us.
- Some mislead us.

But all of them shape the identity we present to the world.

This session helps you explore the influences that formed your beliefs, reactions, behaviors, and emotional patterns.

Not to blame anyone, but to understand yourself more deeply.

Understanding creates freedom.

> *You cannot claim your identity*
> *until you know who helped shape it.*

Insights

In this chapter, the wall challenges the narrator to examine the voices and forces that influenced him.

The wall teaches:

"You are not only what you think, but you are also what has been spoken into you."

The narrator realizes:

1. Some of his thoughts were never his own.

2. Some of his fears were inherited.

3. Some of his behaviors were learned responses to pain.

4. Some of his values were absorbed rather than chosen.

The lecture is about recognizing that influence is powerful and that taking ownership of your life means choosing which influences to keep and which to let go.

> *You have the right to reshape what shaped you.*

REFLECTION QUESTIONS

Answer honestly. This is a moment of discovery, not judgment.

1. Who had the greatest influence on your identity growing up?

____

____

2. What messages did you receive about who you should be?

____

____

3. What messages did you receive about who you were not allowed to be?

____

____

4. What habits or reactions do you now recognize came from someone else's influence?

____

____

5. What influence from your past do you want to release?

____

____

6. What influence from your past do you want to honor or carry forward?

____

____

Personal Exercise
"The Influences That Shaped Me"

This exercise helps you see how your past shaped your present identity.

Step 1: Draw two columns:

Column A: Influences that shaped me in limiting ways.

Examples:

- A critical voice
- A lack of support
- Fear-based teachings
- Expectations to be strong, quiet, tough, invisible

Column B: Influences that shaped me in empowering ways.

Examples:

- Encouragement
- Wisdom
- Resilience
- Someone who believed in you
- Moments of honesty or kindness

Fill each column with real influences from your life.

Column A: Limiting	Column B: Empowering

STEP 2: CHOOSE ONE INFLUENCE FROM COLUMN A.

Finish this sentence:

"This influence impacted me by..."

Write 3–5 sentences.

____

____

____

____

____

____

STEP 3: CHOOSE ONE INFLUENCE FROM COLUMN B.

Finish this sentence:

"This influence taught me that I am..."

Write 3–5 sentences.

____

____

____

____

____

____

____

Both truths matter. Both helped shape the person you are becoming.

YOUR BREAKTHROUGH STATEMENT

Use this prompt:

"I now choose which influences will continue shaping my life. Today, I choose…"

Write your insight here:

____

____

____

____

____

____

____

____

____

____

____

____

____

____

____

This becomes your guiding ownership for the week.

THE REALIZATION

Seeing Yourself Without Excuses or Illusions

INTRODUCTION

A realization is a moment when the truth stands in front of you clearly,

not softened,

not hidden,

not filtered through excuses or fear.

It is the moment you finally understand:

- Why you reacted the way you did,
- Why certain patterns are repeated,
- What you were really afraid of, and
- What you must do next to grow.

This session helps you confront the truth about who you have been, not to punish yourself, but to ***free yourself.***

> Realization is honesty without harshness.
> It is clarity without shame.
> It is seeing yourself as you truly are.

Insights

In the story, the narrator experiences a moment of profound clarity.

The wall teaches him:

This chapter reveals that:

- You are not your excuses.
- You are not your old stories.
- You are not your reactions.
- You are not your fears or illusions.
- You are someone capable of truth.
- You are someone capable of change.
- You are someone capable of reclaiming your life.

Realization is not the end. It is the beginning of becoming someone new.

> *"Realization is not the arrival of truth, but the removal of everything that kept you from seeing it."*

Answer with honesty and compassion.

1. What truth about yourself has become clearer in this journey?

____

____

2. What pattern or behavior do you now see differently?

____

____

3. What excuses have you used to protect yourself from this truth?

____

____

4. How does it feel to see yourself more clearly?

____

____

5. What is becoming undeniable about who you are and what you need?

____

____

6. What realization has the power to change your life moving forward?

____

____

Personal Exercise
"The Truth I See Now"

This exercise helps you name the realization that is emerging in your life.

Step 1: Complete this sentence:

"The truth I now realize about myself is…"

Let the words come naturally.

____

____

____

____

____

Step 2: Answer this question:

"What kept me from seeing this truth sooner?"

It may have been fear, pride, shame, habit, or emotional pain.

____

____

____

____

____

STEP 3: FINISH THIS STATEMENT:

"Seeing this truth now allows me to..."

Write 3–5 sentences about what this realization makes possible for your life.

____

____

____

____

____

STEP 4: REFLECTION

Ask yourself:

"How will I honor this realization moving forward?"

Write your answer clearly and courageously.

____

____

____

____

____

____

____

____

____

Your Breakthrough Statement

Use this prompt:

"Today I honor the truth that I now see: ___________________."

Write your statement here:

____

____

____

____

____

____

____

____

____

____

____

____

____

This becomes your guiding clarity for the week.

The Lesson

(Parts 1 & 2 Combined)

Taking Responsibility for Your Inner World

Introduction

There are moments in life when the truth does more than reveal itself. It ***teaches you*** something.

- A lesson is not a punishment.
- A lesson is not a label.
- A lesson is not a reminder of failure.
- A lesson is an opportunity.
- A moment of understanding.
- A message from your past, delivered to your present, so that your future can be different.

This session helps you uncover the lessons your life has been trying to teach you about

- Your choices,
- Your fears,
- Your habits,
- Your relationships,
- Your identity,
- And your potential.

> *"A lesson only becomes powerful when you are ready to receive it."*

INSIGHTS

In this combined chapter, the narrator confronts the truth of his own patterns.

This realization shows that:

- Lessons repeat until they are understood.
- Pain often reveals what you have ignored.
- Patterns show you what needs healing.
- Responsibility gives you power.
- Awareness opens the path forward.

The narrator begins to see that he cannot grow if he keeps defending his patterns or blaming his environment. He must take ownership of his inner world.

Responsibility is not blame. It is power.

The lesson is this:

You are responsible for your healing, your choices, and your transformation.

> *"Life is always teaching you, but you decide when to learn."*

Take time with these. Let your truth speak through your answers.

1. What lesson has life repeated for you more than once?

____

____

2. What behavior or reaction keeps showing up in your life?

____

____

3. What has that pattern been trying to teach you?

____

____

4. What part of you resisted learning this lesson until now?

____

____

5. What changes might happen if you fully accepted this lesson?

____

____

6. What lesson are you finally ready to stop avoiding?

____

____

PERSONAL EXERCISE
"THE LESSON I NEEDED"

This exercise helps you name the lesson your life has been offering you again and again.

STEP 1: WRITE DOWN ONE DIFFICULT EXPERIENCE OR REPEATED PATTERN IN YOUR LIFE.

It could be:

- A relationship pattern
- A reaction you regret
- A wound you carried for years
- A repeated mistake
- A fear that keeps returning

____

"What was this experience trying to teach me?"

Write the lesson in one clear sentence.

____

____

____

____

____

____

____

____

STEP 3: NOW ANSWER THIS QUESTION:

"Why was it hard for me to learn this lesson before?"

Be honest about the emotions, fears, and beliefs that stood in the way.

____

____

____

____

____

____

____

____

Finish this sentence:

"If I accept this lesson now, my life will begin to change because..."

(Write 4–6 sentences.)

This is your moment of ownership.

____

____

____

____

____

____

____

____

____

____

____

____

____

____

____

YOUR BREAKTHROUGH STATEMENT

Use this prompt:

"The lesson I accept today is ____,
and I choose to grow from it."

Write your statement here:

____

____

____

____

____

____

____

____

____

____

____

____

____

Let this become your truth as you move into the final stages of transformation.

THE REBELLION

Choosing to Break Free from Old Patterns and Identities

INTRODUCTION

Rebellion, in the context of inner work, is not about anger or defiance. It is about **refusing to live the way you used to live.**

It is the moment you say:

- *"I will not repeat this pattern."*
- *"I am done with this old identity."*
- *"I will no longer be controlled by my past."*
- *"I choose something different... something true."*

Rebellion is the powerful act of breaking away from:

- The illusions you once believed
- The roles you once performed
- The walls you once built
- The expectations you once obeyed

This session helps you identify the part of your identity that is ready to break free, and the truth you will replace it with.

This is one of the most empowering sessions in the guide.

In the story, the narrator reaches a turning point.

The wall challenges him to stop accepting the *"old rules"* of his life.

This chapter reveals that:

- Rebellion is not hatred; it is liberation.
- Rebellion is not chaos; it is awakening.
- Rebellion is not running away; it is choosing a new direction.
- Rebellion is the birth of a new identity.

The narrator realizes he no longer needs to conform to the shape others created for him.

The rebellion is internal.

It is the moment he claims himself.

Freedom begins the moment you stop asking permission to be who you are.

> *"Rebellion begins the moment you refuse*
> *to be who the world told you to be."*

Reflection Questions

Answer honestly. This is your moment of truth.

1. What old identity or label are you ready to break away from?

____

____

2. What belief or limitation no longer fits who you are becoming?

____

____

3. What behavior or pattern must you rebel against to grow?

____

____

4. What fears show up when you imagine breaking free?

____

____

5. What part of your true self is waiting to be expressed?

____

____

6. What would your life look like if you fully embraced this inner rebellion?

____

____

Personal Exercise
"My Rebellion Statement"

This exercise helps you boldly declare what you are breaking free from.

Step 1: Write down one belief, behavior, or identity you are ready to break away from.

Examples:

- *"The belief that I'm not enough."*
- *"The habit of pretending I don't care."*
- *"The identity of being the tough one."*
- *"The expectation to hide my feelings."*
- *"The pattern of self-sabotage."*

____

____

____

____

Step 2: Answer this question:

"Why am I rebelling against this now?"

Be honest and direct.

____

____

____

____

STEP 3: WRITE A DECLARATION BEGINNING WITH:

"I refuse to be…"

Let the truth speak.

____

____

____

STEP 4: REFLECTION

Finish this sentence:

"My rebellion will allow me to become…"

Write 4–6 sentences about the new identity you are choosing.

____

____

____

____

____

____

____

____

____

____

____

____

Your Breakthrough Statement

Use this prompt:

"Today I rebel against ____,

so I can become _____________________________________."

Write your declaration here:

____

____

____

____

____

____

____

____

____

____

____

____

This becomes your guiding power for the week.

SESSION 15

THE RESOLVE

Committing to the Life You Choose to Build

INTRODUCTION

Resolve is the moment where clarity becomes commitment.

It is the moment you decide:

- *"I am ready."*
- *"I am able."*
- *"I am willing."*
- *"I choose the life I am becoming."*

Resolve is not perfection.
Resolve is not pressure.
Resolve is not fear disguised as discipline.

Resolve is a **quiet strength** that rises in you when you finally understand:

- Who you are,
- What you want,
- What you no longer accept,
- And where you are headed.

This final session brings together everything you've discovered in this guide: your truth, your awareness, your awakening, your responsibility, your lesson, your rebellion, your identity, and your new direction.

> *Resolve is the beginning of the next chapter in life.*

At the end of the story, the narrator reaches a quiet but powerful understanding.

He realizes:

- His past does not define his future.
- His walls do not define his identity.
- His patterns do not define his potential.
- His awakening has given him a new path.
- The narrator understands that he is free to choose:
- The beliefs he will carry forward,
- The identity he will embody,
- The values he will honor,
- And the life he will build from this moment on.

Resolve is not the end of his story.

Resolve is the beginning of who he becomes.

> *"Resolve is shaping your foundation to support the life you choose to build."*

REFLECTION QUESTIONS

Answer these questions with clarity, courage, and honesty.

1. What is the most important truth you discovered about yourself in this journey?

____

____

2. What is one pattern or belief you commit to releasing permanently?

____

____

3. What value or priority will guide you from this point forward?

____

____

4. Who are you choosing to become? Describe this version of yourself.

____

____

5. What inner strength do you now recognize that you didn't see before?

____

____

6. What does resolve mean to you personally?

____

____

Personal Exercise
"My Life of Resolve"

This final exercise helps you establish your new direction.

Step 1: Write a declaration beginning with:

"From this day forward, I choose to..."

Let this be specific, personal, and powerful.

____

____

____

____

____

Step 2: Answer this question:

"What actions will support the life I am choosing?"

Write 3–5 concrete actions (internal or external).

____

____

____

____

____

STEP 3: NOW WRITE:

"What I will no longer accept from myself is..."

This clarifies your boundaries and commitments.

____

____

____

____

____

____

____

____

Finish with:

"My resolve is strong because I now understand..."

Write 4–8 sentences from your heart.

This is your defining moment.

Your Breakthrough Statement

Use this prompt:

"My resolve is to become

____, and I will

honor this truth every day."

Write your final statement here:

____

____

____

____

____

____

____

____

____

____

____

____

____

____

This becomes the anchor for your next chapter.

In Closing

Your Personal Declaration of Change

You have walked through honesty, awareness, awakening, responsibility, and transformation.

You have faced your past, challenged your beliefs, questioned your illusions, reclaimed your identity, and stepped into resolve.

Now, you will put your journey into words.

This declaration is not for the world; it is for **you**:

Your truth,
Your commitment,
Your transformation,
Your next chapter.

Write slowly.
Write boldly.
Write honestly.

Complete the following statements:

1. "The truth I discovered about myself is…"

2. "The identity I am releasing is…"

3. *"The person I am becoming is..."*

____

____

4. *"The values I choose to honor moving forward are..."*

____

____

5. *"My life will change because I now commit to..."*

____

____

6. Final Declaration:

"From this day forward, I refuse to be just another brick in the wall because..."

____

____

Sign and date below only if you choose to:

Signature: ____________________________

Date: ____________________________

This is your declaration,
your promise to yourself,
your commitment to growth,
your moment of transformation.

Affirmations for the Journey Ahead

Read these affirmations slowly. Return to them whenever you need strength, clarity, or grounding.

Identity

- I am not defined by my past.
- I am allowed to change.
- My story is still being written.

Awareness

- I recognize my truth without fear.
- I see myself with honesty and compassion.
- Awareness gives me power.

Healing

- I release what no longer serves me.
- I forgive myself for what I did not know.
- I allow myself to grow.

Strength

- I choose courage over comfort.
- I stand on the foundation I am building.
- I honor the strength that lives within me.

Purpose

- I am becoming who I was meant to be.
- My life has meaning and direction.
- I walk forward with clarity and resolve.

Choose one affirmation to repeat daily:

"The affirmation I choose to carry with me is:"

____

____

____

____

____

____

____

____

Next Steps You Choose For Your Life

Transformation does not end with the final page of this guide. It continues through the choices you make each day.

Reflect on what steps will support your growth from here.

1. One emotional step I will take is:

____

2. One mental or mindset shift I will work on is:

____

3. One behavioral change I will commit to is:

____

4. One relationship or boundary I will strengthen is:

____

5. One positive habit I will begin is:

____

6. One long-term goal I am now ready to pursue is:

____

These steps do not have to be perfect.

They simply need to be **_intentional._**

Final Reflections

Use the space below for extended thoughts, reflections, dreams, goals, prayers, or insights that arise after completing this guide.

Reflection 1

Reflection 2

Reflection 3

Reflection 4

Reflection 5

Reflection 6

Acknowledgements

This guide is for anyone who has ever struggled to understand themselves, their past, or their purpose.

To the individuals working toward transformation—whether in prison, reentry programs, or personal development circles—thank you for your courage, your honesty, and your willingness to grow.

To the mentors, educators, chaplains, counselors, and group facilitators who support this work, thank you for believing in human potential and in the power of storytelling and transformation.

And to every reader:

Thank you for honoring your truth and stepping into your next chapter.

About the Author

Dirrick L. Williams, Sr. is a writer, speaker, and transformative thought leader whose work centers on identity, truth, and the power of self-reclamation.

His writing blends spiritual clarity, emotional insight, and grounded practicality, inviting readers into a deeper understanding of themselves and the world around them.

With a passion for reaching underserved and overlooked communities, including incarcerated individuals and those navigating major life transitions, Williams creates work that is both reflective and empowering.

His mission is simple:

To help others break free from the stories that limit them, so they may step boldly into the identity they were meant to become.

Learn more by joining our growing community at:

www.livebeyondthewall.com

Subscribe to the podcast at:

https://dontbejustanotherbrickinthewall.podbean.com/

Or contact us at:

www.dirrickwilliams.com

RESOURCES

If you wish to continue your journey of personal growth, identity exploration, or emotional transformation, consider exploring:

- ***Don't Be Just Another Brick in the Wall***, the original work that inspired this guide.
- Reentry and transformation programs in your local community.
- Meditation or mindfulness practices that support emotional awareness.
- Trusted mentors, counselors, or spiritual leaders.
- Writing or journaling as a way to deepen your understanding of yourself.

For Your Notes

For Your Notes

FOR YOUR NOTES